Pretzels at Home!

Delicious Pretzel Variations for You to Try!

BY: Valeria Ray

License Notes

Table of Contents

Introduction

Crispy, fluffy and full of carb-y goodness! Pretzels are for some of the best snack food. But why stop there? Pretzels for dinner? Yes please! This recipe book brings you a medley of sweet and savory pretzels that can be made anytime, anywhere! So let's dive right in!

Basic Soft Pretzels

This is a quick and easy pretzel recipe, perfect for evening snack or a late night delight!

Total Time: 2h 20m

Serves: 8

Ingredients:

- 1 package active dry yeast
- 1 cup warm water
- 1 tbsp. brown sugar
- 3 ¼ cups bread flour
- ½ cup cold beer
- 2 tbsp. unsalted butter, cut into 1 inch pieces, at room temperature, plus more for greasing
- 2 tsp salt

Instructions:

1. Preheat oven to 500 F.

2. Into a stand mixer, add in the warm water. Sprinkle on the yeast

3. Add in the brown sugar. Mix thoroughly and allow to bloom until foamy. This should take about 5 minutes.

4. Add in the flour, butter, salt, and beer, and continue stirring. On low speed, begin kneading the dough for a minute or until it forms a smooth ball. Continue kneading until the dough become pliant – about 5 minutes.

5. In a lightly greased bowl, place dough and cover with saran wrap. Set away to rise in a warm area for 90 minutes, until double.

6. Divide into 8 portions and roll out into desired shape – knots, buns, or sticks.

7. Arrange on 2 lined baking trays about 2 inches apart.

8. Allow to rise for 30 more minutes.

9. Coat with a quick egg wash before baking for 8-10 minutes until crispy and golden brown!

Whole Wheat Pretzels

Want a healthier option? Try this whole wheat pretzel recipe instead!

Total Time: 2h 15m

Serves: 8

Ingredients:

- 1 package active dry yeast
- 1 cup warm water
- 1 tbsp. brown sugar
- 2 cups bread flour
- 1 ¼ cup whole wheat flour
- ½ cup cold beer
- 2 tbsp. unsalted butter, cut into 1 inch pieces, at room temperature, plus more for greasing
- 2 tsp salt

Instructions:

1. Preheat oven to 500 F.

2. Into a stand mixer, add in the warm water. Sprinkle on the yeast

3. Add in the brown sugar. Mix thoroughly and allow to bloom until foamy. This should take about 5 minutes.

4. Add in the flours, butter, salt, and beer, and continue stirring. On low speed, begin kneading the dough for a minute or until it forms a smooth ball. Continue kneading until the dough become pliant – about 5 minutes.

5. In a lightly greased bowl, place dough and cover with saran wrap. Set away to rise in a warm area for 90 minutes, until double.

6. Divide into 8 portions and roll out into desired shape – knots, buns, or sticks.

7. Arrange on 2 lined baking trays about 2 inches apart.

8. Allow to rise for 30 more minutes.

9. Coat with a quick egg wash before baking for 8-10 minutes until crispy and golden brown!

Spelt Pretzels

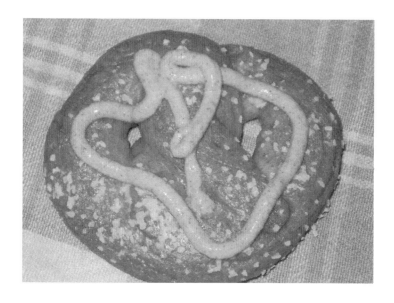

Another spin off, this recipe uses spelt flour to make delicious soft pretzels!

Total Time: 2h 10m

Serves: 8

Ingredients:

- 1 package active dry yeast
- 1 cup warm water
- 1 tbsp. brown sugar
- 2 cups bread flour
- 1 ¼ cup spelt flour
- ½ cup cold beer
- 2 tbsp. unsalted butter, cut into 1 inch pieces, at room temperature, plus more for greasing
- 2 tsp salt

Instructions:

1. Preheat oven to 500 F.

2. Into a stand mixer, add in the warm water. Sprinkle on the yeast

3. Add in the brown sugar. Mix thoroughly and allow to bloom until foamy. This should take about 5 minutes.

4. Add in the flour, butter, salt, and beer, and continue stirring. On low speed, begin kneading the dough for a minute or until it forms a smooth ball. Continue kneading until the dough become pliant – about 5 minutes.

5. In a lightly greased bowl, place dough and cover with saran wrap. Set away to rise in a warm area for 90 minutes, until double.

6. Divide into 8 portions and roll out into desired shape – knots, buns, or sticks.

7. Arrange on 2 lined baking trays about 2 inches apart.

8. Allow to rise for 30 more minutes.

9. Coat with a quick egg wash before baking for 8-10 minutes until crispy and golden brown!

Olive and Garlic Pretzels

Let's get fancy with this delicious olive and garlic pretzel recipe!

Total Time: 2h 20m

Serves: 8

Ingredients:

- 1 package active dry yeast
- 1 cup warm water
- 1 tbsp. brown sugar
- 2 cups bread flour
- 1 ¼ cup spelt flour
- 1/3 cup cold beer
- 2 tbsp. unsalted butter, cut into 1 inch pieces, at room temperature
- 2 tsp salt
- ½ cup pitted olives, roughly chopped
- 1 tbsp. garlic, minced
- 1 tbsp. fresh thyme, chopped
- ½ cup crumbled feta

Instructions:

1. Preheat oven to 500 F.

2. Into a stand mixer, add in the warm water. Sprinkle on the yeast

3. Add in the brown sugar. Mix thoroughly and allow to bloom until foamy. This should take about 5 minutes.

4. Add in the flour, butter, salt, and beer, and continue stirring. On low speed, begin kneading the dough for a minute or until it forms a smooth ball.

5. Add in the olives, garlic, and thyme and continue kneading until the dough become pliant – about 5 minutes.

6. In a lightly greased bowl, place dough and cover with saran wrap. Set away to rise in a warm area for 90 minutes, until double.

7. Divide into 8 portions and roll out into desired shape – knots, buns, or sticks.

8. Arrange on 2 lined baking trays about 2 inches apart.

9. Allow to rise for 30 more minutes.

10. Coat with a quick egg wash before baking for 8-10 minutes until crispy and golden brown!

11. Serve with crumbled feta!

Cinnamon-Raisin Pretzels

Looking for something sweet without going over the top? These cinnamon raisin pretzels are perfect with a cup of coffee!

Total Time: 2h 30m

Serves: 8

Ingredients:

- 1 package active dry yeast
- 1 cup + 2 tbsp. warm water
- 1 tbsp. brown sugar
- 2 cups bread flour
- 1 ¼ cup spelt flour
- 2 tbsp. unsalted butter, cut into 1 inch pieces, at room temperature, plus more for greasing
- ½ tsp salt
- ½ cup raisins
- 3 tbsp. cinnamon powder
- 2 tbsp. sugar + 1 tsp cinnamon.

Instructions:

1. Preheat oven to 500 F.

2. Into a stand mixer, add in the warm water. Sprinkle on the yeast

3. Add in the brown sugar. Mix thoroughly and allow to bloom until foamy. This should take about 5 minutes.

4. Add in the flour, butter, salt, and beer, and continue stirring. On low speed, begin kneading the dough for a minute or until it forms a smooth ball.

5. Add in the raisins and cinnamon powder and continue kneading until the dough become pliant – about 5 minutes.

6. In a lightly greased bowl, place dough and cover with saran wrap. Set away to rise in a warm area for 90 minutes, until double.

7. Divide into 8 portions and roll out into desired shape – knots, buns, or sticks.

8. Arrange on 2 lined baking trays about 2 inches apart.

9. Allow to rise for 30 more minutes.

10. Coat with a quick egg wash and sprinkle with sugar and cinnamon mixture before baking for 8-10 minutes until crispy and golden brown!

Cheesy Jalapeno Pretzel Bites

Gooey melty cheese awaits you inside these pretzel bites!

Total Time: 2h 40m

Serves: 12

Ingredients:

- 1 package active dry yeast
- 1 cup warm water
- 1 tbsp. brown sugar
- 3 ¼ cups bread flour
- ½ cup cold beer
- 2 tbsp. unsalted butter, cut into 1 inch pieces, at room temperature, plus more for greasing
- 2 tsp salt
- 2 cups grated cheddar
- 2 jalapeno peppers, sliced thinly
- Coarse salt for topping

Instructions:

1. Preheat oven to 500 F.

2. Into a stand mixer, add in the warm water. Sprinkle on the yeast

3. Add in the brown sugar. Mix thoroughly and allow to bloom until foamy. This should take about 5 minutes.

4. Add in the flour, butter, salt, and beer, and continue stirring. On low speed, begin kneading the dough for a minute or until it forms a smooth ball. Continue kneading until the dough become pliant – about 5 minutes.

5. In a lightly greased bowl, place dough and cover with saran wrap. Set away to rise in a warm area for 90 minutes, until double.

6. Place dough on a floured counter and divide into 12 equal portions.

7. Roll each piece into a rectangle. Place a line of cheese in the center (about 2 tbsp.) and top with a 3-4 jalapeno slices.

8. Pull the two edges of the dough together and pinch to cover. Ensure the cheese is completely covered and set onto a baking tray.

9. Repeat with the rest of the cheese and dough. Place dough pieces 2 inches apart.

10. Allow to rise for 30 more minutes.

11. Coat with a quick egg wash before baking for 8-10 minutes until crispy and golden brown!

12. Top with coarse salt before serving!

Peanut Butter Pretzel Bites

Who doesn't love peanut butter? Add in soft pretzel bites and you have a winning recipe!

Total Time: 2h 30m

Serves: 12

Ingredients:

- 1 package active dry yeast
- 1 cup warm water
- 1 tbsp. brown sugar
- 3 ¼ cups bread flour
- ½ cup cold beer
- 2 tbsp. unsalted butter, cut into 1 inch pieces, at room temperature, plus more for greasing
- 2 tsp salt
- 1 ½ cups creamy peanut butter

Instructions:

1. Preheat oven to 500 F.

2. Into a stand mixer, add in the warm water. Sprinkle on the yeast

3. Add in the brown sugar. Mix thoroughly and allow to bloom until foamy. This should take about 5 minutes.

4. Add in the flour, butter, salt, and beer, and continue stirring. On low speed, begin kneading the dough for a minute or until it forms a smooth ball. Continue kneading until the dough become pliant – about 5 minutes.

5. In a lightly greased bowl, place dough and cover with saran wrap. Set away to rise in a warm area for 90 minutes, until double.

6. Place dough on a floured counter and divide into 12 equal portions.

7. Roll each piece into a rectangle. Place a line of peanut butter in the center (about 2 tbsp.)

8. Pull the two edges of the dough together and pinch to cover. Ensure the filling is completely covered and set onto a baking tray.

9. Repeat with the rest of the filling and dough. Place dough pieces 2 inches apart.

10. Allow to rise for 30 more minutes.

11. Coat with a quick egg wash before baking for 8-10 minutes until crispy and golden brown!

Nutella Pretzel Bites

Picky eaters are guaranteed to enjoy this delicious Nutella filled pretzel bites recipes!

Total Time: 2h 20m

Serves: 12

Ingredients:

- 1 package active dry yeast
- 1 cup warm water
- 1 tbsp. brown sugar
- 3 ¼ cups bread flour
- ½ cup cold beer
- 2 tbsp. unsalted butter, cut into 1 inch pieces, at room temperature, plus more for greasing
- 2 tsp salt
- 1 ½ cups Nutella
- 4 tbsp. chopped hazelnuts

Instructions:

1. Preheat oven to 500 F.

2. Into a stand mixer, add in the warm water. Sprinkle on the yeast

3. Add in the brown sugar. Mix thoroughly and allow to bloom until foamy. This should take about 5 minutes.

4. Add in the flour, butter, salt, and beer, and continue stirring. On low speed, begin kneading the dough for a minute or until it forms a smooth ball. Continue kneading until the dough become pliant – about 5 minutes.

5. In a lightly greased bowl, place dough and cover with saran wrap. Set away to rise in a warm area for 90 minutes, until double.

6. Place dough on a floured counter and divide into 12 equal portions.

7. Roll each piece into a rectangle. Place a line of nutella in the center (about 2 tbsp.) and top with a tsp of crushed hazelnuts.

8. Pull the two edges of the dough together and pinch to cover. Ensure the nutella is completely covered and set onto a baking tray.

9. Repeat with rest of the filling and dough. Place dough pieces 2 inches apart.

10. Allow to rise for 30 more minutes.

11. Coat with a quick egg wash before baking for 8-10 minutes until crispy and golden brown!

Coconut Cream Cheese Pretzel Bites

These pretzel bites are brilliants for an evening tea!

Total Time: 2h 40m

Serves: 12

Ingredients:

- 1 package active dry yeast
- 1 cup warm water
- 1 tbsp. brown sugar
- 3 ¼ cups bread flour
- ½ cup cold milk
- 2 tbsp. unsalted butter, cut into 1 inch pieces, at room temperature, plus more for greasing
- 2 tsp salt
- 1 ½ cups cream cheese frosting
- 4 tbsp. coconut flakes
- Sweetened coconut flakes for topping

Instructions:

1. Preheat oven to 500 F.

2. Into a stand mixer, add in the warm water. Sprinkle on the yeast

3. Add in the brown sugar. Mix thoroughly and allow to bloom until foamy. This should take about 5 minutes.

4. Add in the flour, butter, salt, and milk, and continue stirring. On low speed, begin kneading the dough for a minute or until it forms a smooth ball. Continue kneading until the dough become pliant – about 5 minutes.

5. In a lightly greased bowl, place dough and cover with saran wrap. Set away to rise in a warm area for 90 minutes, until double.

6. Place dough on a floured counter and divide into 12 equal portions.

7. Roll each piece into a rectangle. Place a line of frosting in the center (about 2 tbsp.) and top with a tsp of coconut flakes.

8. Pull the two edges of the dough together and pinch to cover. Ensure the filling is completely covered and set onto a baking tray.

9. Repeat with rest of the filling and dough. Place dough pieces 2 inches apart.

10. Allow to rise for 30 more minutes.

11. Coat with a quick egg wash before baking for 8-10 minutes until crispy and golden brown!

12. Top with sweetened coconut flakes if desired before serving!

Cheesy Garlic Pull Apart Pretzels

Looking for game night recipes? Whip up these delicious pretzel pull aparts!

Total Time: 2h 30m

Serves: 12

Ingredients:

- 1 package active dry yeast
- 1 cup warm water
- 1 tbsp. brown sugar
- 3 ¼ cups bread flour
- ½ cup cold milk
- 2 tbsp. unsalted butter, cut into 1 inch pieces, at room temperature, plus more for greasing
- 2 tsp salt
- 24 bocconcini mozzarella balls
- 1 tbsp unsalted butter, melted
- 3 tbsp chopped garlic
- 3 tbsp chopped fresh flat-leaf parsley

Instructions:

1. Preheat oven to 500 F.

2. Into a stand mixer, add in the warm water. Sprinkle on the yeast

3. Add in the brown sugar. Mix thoroughly and allow to bloom until foamy. This should take about 5 minutes.

4. Add in the flour, butter, salt, and beer, and continue stirring. On low speed, begin kneading the dough for a minute or until it forms a smooth ball. Continue kneading until the dough become pliant – about 5 minutes.

5. In a lightly greased bowl, place dough and cover with saran wrap. Set away to rise in a warm area for 90 minutes, until double.

6. Place dough on a floured counter and divide into 12 equal portions.

7. Roll each piece into a 4 inch circle.

8. Tear two of the mozzarella balls in half and pile them in the center of the dough.

9. Pinch together edges of dough to cover. Ensure the cheese is completely covered. Roll in your palms to ensure a proper sphere shape and set onto a lined baking tray.

10. Repeat with the rest of the cheese and dough. Place dough pieces 2 inches apart.

11. Allow to rise for 30 more minutes before baking for 5 minutes.

12. Remove from oven and coat with the melted butter and sprinkle with garlic.

13. Bake again for 5 minutes until crispy and golden brown.

14. Remove from oven and top with parsley before serving!

Caramel Pretzel Bites

Soft lush bread with a gooey Caramel centre? Sign us up!

Total Time: 2h 20m

Serves: 12

Ingredients:

- 1 package active dry yeast
- 1 cup warm water
- 1 tbsp. brown sugar
- 3 ¼ cups bread flour
- ½ cup cold milk
- 2 tbsp. unsalted butter, cut into 1 inch pieces, at room temperature, plus more for greasing
- 2 tsp salt
- 1 ½ cups store bought caramel sauce

Instructions:

1. Preheat oven to 500 F.

2. Into a stand mixer, add in the warm water. Sprinkle on the yeast

3. Add in the brown sugar. Mix thoroughly and allow to bloom until foamy. This should take about 5 minutes.

4. Add in the flour, butter, salt, and beer, and continue stirring. On low speed, begin kneading the dough for a minute or until it forms a smooth ball. Continue kneading until the dough become pliant – about 5 minutes.

5. In a lightly greased bowl, place dough and cover with saran wrap. Set away to rise in a warm area for 90 minutes, until double.

6. Place dough on a floured counter and divide into 12 equal portions.

7. Roll each piece into a rectangle. Place about 2 tbsp. of caramel sauce in the center.

8. Pull the two edges of the dough together and pinch to cover. Ensure the caramel is completely covered and set onto a baking tray.

9. Repeat with the rest of the dough. Place dough pieces 2 inches apart.

10. Allow to rise for 30 more minutes.

11. Coat with a quick egg wash before baking for 8-10 minutes until crispy and golden brown!

Pizza Pretzel Bites

This recipe combines classic pizza flavours inside a soft and fluffy pretzel!

Total Time: 2h 20m

Serves: 12

Ingredients:

- 1 package active dry yeast
- 1 cup warm water
- 1 tbsp. brown sugar
- 3 ¼ cups bread flour
- ½ cup cold beer
- 2 tbsp. unsalted butter, cut into 1 inch pieces, at room temperature, plus more for greasing
- 2 tsp salt
- 1 cup pizza sauce
- 2 tbsp. olives, chopped
- ½ cup grated cheese

Instructions:

1. Preheat oven to 500 F.

2. Into a stand mixer, add in the warm water. Sprinkle on the yeast

3. Add in the brown sugar. Mix thoroughly and allow to bloom until foamy. This should take about 5 minutes.

4. Add in the flour, butter, salt, and beer, and continue stirring. On low speed, begin kneading the dough for a minute or until it forms a smooth ball. Continue kneading until the dough become pliant – about 5 minutes.

5. In a lightly greased bowl, place dough and cover with saran wrap. Set away to rise in a warm area for 90 minutes, until double.

6. In the meantime, combine the pizza sauce and olives. Set aside.

7. Place dough on a floured counter and divide into 12 equal portions.

8. Roll out one portion into a rectangle. Place a heap of pizza sauce mixture in the center (about 2 tbsp.) and top with a tsp of grated cheese.

9. Pull the two edges of the dough together and pinch to cover. Ensure the filling is completely covered and set onto a baking tray.

10. Repeat with the rest of the dough. Place dough pieces 2 inches apart.

11. Allow to rise for 30 more minutes.

12. Coat with a quick egg wash before baking for 8-10 minutes until crispy and golden brown!

Pretzeldogs

A classic appetizer, these pretzeldogs are loved by adults and children alike!

Total Time: 2h 20m

Serves: 24

Ingredients:

- 1 package active dry yeast
- 1 cup warm water
- 1 tbsp. brown sugar
- 3 ¼ cups bread flour
- ½ cup cold beer
- 2 tbsp. unsalted butter, cut into 1 inch pieces, at room temperature, plus more for greasing
- 2 tsp salt
- 6 hotdogs, cut into 1 inch pieces.

Instructions:

1. Preheat oven to 500 F.

2. Into a stand mixer, add in the warm water. Sprinkle on the yeast

3. Add in the brown sugar. Mix thoroughly and allow to bloom until foamy. This should take about 5 minutes.

4. Add in the flour, butter, salt, and beer, and continue stirring. On low speed, begin kneading the dough for a minute or until it forms a smooth ball. Continue kneading until the dough become pliant – about 5 minutes.

5. In a lightly greased bowl, place dough and cover with saran wrap. Set away to rise in a warm area for 90 minutes, until double.

6. Place dough on a floured counter and divide into 12 equal portions. Further divide each portion into 2 for a total of 24 pieces.

7. Roll out one portion into a rectangle. Place one piece of hotdog in the center and pull the two edges of the dough together. Pinch to cover. Ensure the hotdog is completely covered and set onto a baking tray.

8. Repeat with the rest of the cheese and dough. Place dough pieces 2 inches apart.

9. Allow to rise for 30 more minutes.

10. Coat with a quick egg wash before baking for 8-10 minutes until crispy and golden brown!

Parmesan Crusted Soft Pretzels

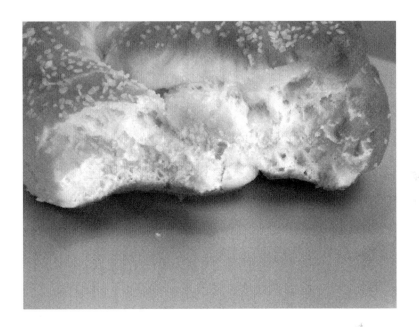

You no longer need to head to the mall to get your favourite parmesan pretzels. With this easy recipe, you can now make it yourself!

Total Time: 2h 20m

Serves: 8

Ingredients:

- 1 package active dry yeast
- 1 cup warm water
- 1 tbsp. brown sugar
- 3 ¼ cups bread flour
- ½ cup cold milk
- 2 tbsp. unsalted butter, cut into 1 inch pieces, at room temperature, plus more for greasing
- 2 tsp salt
- 1 cup grated parmesan cheese

Instructions:

1. Preheat oven to 500 F.

2. Into a stand mixer, add in the warm water. Sprinkle on the yeast

3. Add in the brown sugar. Mix thoroughly and allow to bloom until foamy. This should take about 5 minutes.

4. Add in the flour, butter, salt, and milk, and continue stirring. On low speed, begin kneading the dough for a minute or until it forms a smooth ball. Continue kneading until the dough become pliant – about 5 minutes.

5. In a lightly greased bowl, place dough and cover with saran wrap. Set away to rise in a warm area for 90 minutes, until double.

6. Divide into 8 portions and roll out into desired shape – knots, buns, or sticks.

7. Arrange on 2 lined baking trays about 2 inches apart.

8. Allow to rise for 30 more minutes.

9. Coat with a quick egg wash and sprinkle with grated parmesan before baking for 8-10 minutes until crispy and golden brown!

10. Serve warm!

Chocolate Pretzels

This chocolate pretzels are perfect for a children's get-together party!

Total Time: 2h 20m

Serves: 8

Ingredients:

- 1 package active dry yeast
- 1 cup warm water
- 1 tbsp. brown sugar
- 2 ½ cups bread flour
- ¾ cup cocoa
- ½ cup cold milk
- 2 tbsp. unsalted butter, cut into 1 inch pieces, at room temperature, plus more for greasing
- 2 tsp salt
- ¾ cups white chocolate chips

Instructions:

1. Preheat oven to 500 F.

2. Into a stand mixer, add in the warm water. Sprinkle on the yeast

3. Add in the brown sugar. Mix thoroughly and allow to bloom until foamy. This should take about 5 minutes.

4. Add in the flour, cocoa, butter, salt, and milk, and continue stirring. On low speed, begin kneading the dough for a minute or until it forms a smooth ball.

5. Add in the chocolate chips and continue kneading until the dough become pliant – about 5 minutes.

6. In a lightly greased bowl, place dough and cover with saran wrap. Set away to rise in a warm area for 90 minutes, until double.

7. Divide into 8 portions and roll out into desired shape – knots, buns, or sticks.

8. Arrange on 2 lined baking trays about 2 inches apart.

9. Allow to rise for 30 more minutes.

10. Bake for 8-10 minutes until crispy!

11. Serve warm!

Choco Dipped Pretzels

Pretzels and gooey molten chocolate? Delicious!

Total Time: 2h 20m

Serves: 8

Ingredients:

- 1 package active dry yeast
- 1 cup warm water
- 1 tbsp. brown sugar
- 3 ¼ cups bread flour
- ½ cup cold beer
- 2 tbsp. unsalted butter, cut into 1 inch pieces, at room temperature, plus more for greasing
- 2 tsp salt
- 1 cup chocolate chips
- 1 tbsp butter

Instructions:

1. Preheat oven to 500 F.

2. Into a stand mixer, add in the warm water. Sprinkle on the yeast

3. Add in the brown sugar. Mix thoroughly and allow to bloom until foamy. This should take about 5 minutes.

4. Add in the flour, butter, salt, and beer, and continue stirring. On low speed, begin kneading the dough for a minute or until it forms a smooth ball. Continue kneading until the dough become pliant – about 5 minutes.

5. In a lightly greased bowl, place dough and cover with saran wrap. Set away to rise in a warm area for 90 minutes, until double.

6. Divide into 8 portions and roll out into desired shape – knots, buns, or sticks.

7. Arrange on 2 lined baking trays about 2 inches apart.

8. Allow to rise for 30 more minutes.

9. Coat with a quick egg wash before baking for 8-10 minutes until crispy and golden brown!

10. In a saucepan, melt together the chocolate and butter until smooth.

11. To serve, begin dipping pretzels into the chocolate and lay on a wax paper lined tray.

12. Cool for 20 minutes before serving!

Cinnamon Sugar Pretzels

These are a personal favourite! The rich cinnamon flavor perfectly balances the crunchy sweetness of the sugar.

Total Time: 2h 20m

Serves: 8

Ingredients:

- 1 package active dry yeast
- 1 cup warm water
- 1 tbsp. brown sugar
- 3 ¼ cups bread flour
- ½ cup cold beer
- 2 tbsp. unsalted butter, cut into 1 inch pieces, at room temperature, plus more for greasing
- 2 tsp salt
- ½ cup sugar
- ½ tbsp cinnamon
- 1 tbsp butter, melted

Instructions:

1. Preheat oven to 500 F.

2. Into a stand mixer, add in the warm water. Sprinkle on the yeast

3. Add in the brown sugar. Mix thoroughly and allow to bloom until foamy. This should take about 5 minutes.

4. Add in the flour, butter, salt, and beer, and continue stirring. On low speed, begin kneading the dough for a minute or until it forms a smooth ball. Continue kneading until the dough become pliant – about 5 minutes.

5. In a lightly greased bowl, place dough and cover with saran wrap. Set away to rise in a warm area for 90 minutes, until double.

6. Divide into 8 portions and roll out into desired shape – knots, buns, or sticks.

7. Arrange on 2 lined baking trays about 2 inches apart.

8. Allow to rise for 30 more minutes.

9. Coat with a quick egg wash before baking for 8-10 minutes until crispy and golden brown!

10. As the pretzels back, in a small bowl, combine the sugar and cinnamon.

11. Once baked, remove from oven and lightly coat with melted butter while still piping hot. Sprinkle on cinnamon sugar!

12. Serve warm!

Philly Cheesesteak Pretzels

Everyone's favourite sandwich in a pretzel roll? Count us in!

Total Time: 2h 20m

Serves: 8

Ingredients:

- 1 package active dry yeast
- 1 cup warm water
- 1 tbsp. brown sugar
- 3 ¼ cups bread flour
- ½ cup cold beer
- 2 tbsp. unsalted butter, cut into 1 inch pieces, at room temperature, plus more for greasing
- 2 tsp salt

Filling:

- 2 tbsp. olive oil
- 1 green bell pepper, thinly sliced
- 1 onion, thinly sliced
- ½ tsp sea salt
- All-purpose flour for dusting
- 8 oz. thinly sliced roast beef
- 8 slices provolone cheese

Instructions:

1. Preheat oven to 500 F.

2. To make the filling, heat a large pan with the oil. When hot, add in the pepper, onion, and salt. Cook until brown and tender for about 15 minutes.

3. Remove from pan and set aside.

4. Into a stand mixer, add in the warm water. Sprinkle on the yeast

5. Add in the brown sugar. Mix thoroughly and allow to bloom until foamy. This should take about 5 minutes.

6. Add in the flour, butter, salt, and beer, and continue stirring. On low speed, begin kneading the dough for a minute or until it forms a smooth ball. Continue kneading until the dough become pliant – about 5 minutes.

7. In a lightly greased bowl, place dough and cover with saran wrap. Set away to rise in a warm area for 90 minutes, until double.

8. Divide into 8 equal portions and being roll out one piece of dough into a large rectangle. Approximately 6.5 x 7.5 inches.

9. With the shorter end at the bottom, layer on one slice of the beef, 2 tbsp. of onion filling, and a slice of cheese along the lower half. Make sure to leave ½ an inch of dough border around the filling.

10. Fold the top of the dough over and press together the edges. Repeat with the rest of the dough pieces.

11. Arrange on 2 lined baking trays about 2 inches apart.

12. Allow to rise for 30 more minutes.

13. Coat with a quick egg wash before baking for 8-10 minutes until crispy and golden brown!

14. Serve warm!

Cheeseburger Pretzels

Another classic now inside a pretzel! These are great as a starter for a dinner party!

Total Time: 2h 20m

Serves: 8

Ingredients:

- 1 package active dry yeast
- 1 cup warm water
- 1 tbsp. brown sugar
- 3 ¼ cups bread flour
- ½ cup cold beer
- 2 tbsp. unsalted butter, cut into 1 inch pieces, at room temperature, plus more for greasing
- 2 tsp salt

Filling:

- 1 onion, thinly sliced
- ½ tsp sea salt
- 8 oz. cooked minced beef
- 8 slices American cheese
- Pickles, chopped
- Ketchup
- Mustard

Instructions:

1. Preheat oven to 500 F.

2. To make the filling, heat a large pan with the oil. When hot, add in the pepper, onion, and salt. Cook until brown and tender for about 15 minutes.

3. Remove from pan and set aside.

4. Into a stand mixer, add in the warm water. Sprinkle on the yeast

5. Add in the brown sugar. Mix thoroughly and allow to bloom until foamy. This should take about 5 minutes.

6. Add in the flour, butter, salt, and beer, and continue stirring. On low speed, begin kneading the dough for a minute or until it forms a smooth ball. Continue kneading until the dough become pliant – about 5 minutes.

7. In a lightly greased bowl, place dough and cover with saran wrap. Set away to rise in a warm area for 90 minutes, until double.

8. Divide into 8 equal portions and being roll out one piece of dough into a large rectangle. Approximately 6.5 x 7.5 inches.

9. With the shorter end at the bottom, layer on 1 oz. of the cooked beef, 1 tbsp. of onion slices, and a slice of cheese along the lower half. Make sure to leave ½ an inch of dough border around the filling.

10. Top with desired toppings and fold the top of the dough over and press together the edges. Repeat with rest of the dough pieces.

11. Arrange on 2 lined baking trays about 2 inches apart.

12. Allow to rise for 30 more minutes.

13. Coat with a quick egg wash before baking for 8-10 minutes until crispy and golden brown!

14. Serve warm!

Crunchy Pretzel Rods

Make these in advance to have delicious pretzel snacks throughout the week.

Total Time: 1 hour prep + 8 hours resting

Serves: 48 rods

Ingredients:

- 1 package active dry yeast
- 1 cup warm water
- 1 tbsp. brown sugar
- 3 ¼ cups all-purpose flour
- 2 tbsp. unsalted butter, cut into 1 inch pieces, at room temperature, plus more for greasing
- 2 tsp salt

Instructions:

1. Into a stand mixer, add in the warm water. Sprinkle on the yeast

2. Add in the brown sugar. Mix thoroughly and allow to bloom until foamy. This should take about 5 minutes.

3. Add in the flour, butter, and salt, and continue stirring. On low speed, begin kneading the dough for a minute or until it forms a smooth ball. Continue kneading until the dough become pliant – about 5 minutes.

4. In a lightly greased bowl, place dough and cover with saran wrap. Place dough in refrigerator and allow to cold rise for 8 hours or up to 24 hours.

5. Preheat oven to 325 F

6. Divide into 48 equal portions and begin rolling out into a thin long shape.

7. Arrange on 2 lined baking trays about 2 inches apart.

8. Allow to rise on the counter for 30 more minutes.

9. Sprinkle with salt before baking for 20-30 minutes, testing for hardness.

Chocolate Dipped Hard Pretzels

A delicious hard pretzel variation – with CHOCOLATE!

Total Time: 1 hour prep + 8 hours resting

Serves: 48 rods

Ingredients:

- 1 package active dry yeast
- 1 cup warm water
- 1 tbsp. brown sugar
- 3 ¼ cups all-purpose flour
- 2 tbsp. unsalted butter, cut into 1 inch pieces, at room temperature, plus more for greasing
- 2 tsp salt

Instructions:

1. Into a stand mixer, add in the warm water. Sprinkle on the yeast

2. Add in the brown sugar. Mix thoroughly and allow to bloom until foamy. This should take about 5 minutes.

3. Add in the flour, butter, and salt, and continue stirring. On low speed, begin kneading the dough for a minute or until it forms a smooth ball. Continue kneading until the dough become pliant – about 5 minutes.

4. In a lightly greased bowl, place dough and cover with saran wrap. Place dough in refrigerator and allow to cold rise for 8 hours or up to 24 hours.

5. Preheat oven to 325 F

6. Divide into 48 equal portions and begin rolling out into a thin long shape.

7. Arrange on 2 lined baking trays about 2 inches apart.

8. Allow to rise on the counter for 30 more minutes.

9. Sprinkle with salt before baking for 20-30 minutes, testing for hardness.

10. In a saucepan, melt together the chocolate and butter until smooth.

11. To serve, begin dipping pretzels into the chocolate and lay on a wax paper lined tray. You could now top with nuts or sprinkles if desired.

12. Cool for 20 minutes before serving!

Sprinkle Pretzels

Kids are going to absolutely love this! This recipe calls for white chocolate covered with sprinkles!

Total Time: 2h 20m

Serves: 8

Ingredients:

- 1 package active dry yeast
- 1 cup warm water
- 1 tbsp. brown sugar
- 3 ¼ cups bread flour
- ½ cup cold beer
- 2 tbsp. unsalted butter, cut into 1 inch pieces, at room temperature, plus more for greasing
- 2 tsp salt
- 1 cup white chocolate chips
- 1 tbsp butter
- ½ cup sprinkles

Instructions:

1. Preheat oven to 500 F.

2. Into a stand mixer, add in the warm water. Sprinkle on the yeast

3. Add in the brown sugar. Mix thoroughly and allow to bloom until foamy. This should take about 5 minutes.

4. Add in the flour, butter, salt, and beer, and continue stirring. On low speed, begin kneading the dough for a minute or until it forms a smooth ball. Continue kneading until the dough become pliant – about 5 minutes.

5. In a lightly greased bowl, place dough and cover with saran wrap. Set away to rise in a warm area for 90 minutes, until double.

6. Divide into 8 portions and roll out into desired shape – knots, buns, or sticks.

7. Arrange on 2 lined baking trays about 2 inches apart.

8. Allow to rise for 30 more minutes.

9. Coat with a quick egg wash before baking for 8-10 minutes until crispy and golden brown!

10. In a saucepan, melt together the chocolate and butter until smooth.

11. To serve, begin dipping pretzels into the chocolate and lay on a wax paper lined tray. Toss on sprinkles while still wet.

12. Set for 20 minutes before serving!

Cheese Dipped Pretzels

These pretzels are absolutely delicious for game night!

Total Time: 2h 20m

Serves: 8

Ingredients:

- 1 package active dry yeast
- 1 cup warm water
- 1 tbsp. brown sugar
- 3 ¼ cups bread flour
- ½ cup cold beer
- 2 tbsp. unsalted butter, cut into 1 inch pieces, at room temperature, plus more for greasing
- 2 tsp salt
- 1 cup grated cheddar, melted

Instructions:

1. Preheat oven to 500 F.

2. Into a stand mixer, add in the warm water. Sprinkle on the yeast

3. Add in the brown sugar. Mix thoroughly and allow to bloom until foamy. This should take about 5 minutes.

4. Add in the flour, butter, salt, and beer, and continue stirring. On low speed, begin kneading the dough for a minute or until it forms a smooth ball. Continue kneading until the dough become pliant – about 5 minutes.

5. In a lightly greased bowl, place dough and cover with saran wrap. Set away to rise in a warm area for 90 minutes, until double.

6. Divide into 8 portions and roll out into desired shape – knots, buns, or sticks.

7. Arrange on 2 lined baking trays about 2 inches apart.

8. Allow to rise for 30 more minutes.

9. Coat with a quick egg wash before baking for 8-10 minutes until crispy and golden brown!

10. To serve, begin dipping pretzels into the melted cheese and lay on a wax paper lined tray.

11. Set for 20 minutes before serving!

Breakfast Pretzels

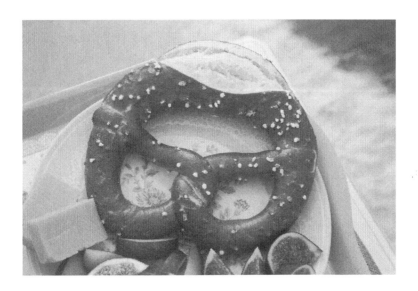

You can make these pretzels the night before and simply pop them into the oven for 5 minutes for a delicious and quick breakfast!

Total Time: 2h 10m

Serves: 8

Ingredients:

- 1 package active dry yeast
- 1 cup warm water
- 1 tbsp. brown sugar
- 2 cups bread flour
- 1 ¼ cup spelt flour
- 1/3 cup cold beer
- 2 tbsp. unsalted butter, cut into 1 inch pieces, at room temperature
- 2 tsp salt
- 1 large tomato, chopped
- ½ cup grated cheddar cheese
- 1 tbsp. fresh basil

Instructions:

1. Preheat oven to 500 F.

2. Into a stand mixer, add in the warm water. Sprinkle on the yeast

3. Add in the brown sugar. Mix thoroughly and allow to bloom until foamy. This should take about 5 minutes.

4. Add in the flour, butter, salt, and beer, and continue stirring. On low speed, begin kneading the dough for a minute or until it forms a smooth ball.

5. Add in the tomato, cheese, and basil and continue kneading until the dough become pliant – about 5 minutes.

6. In a lightly greased bowl, place dough and cover with saran wrap. Set away to rise in a warm area for 90 minutes, until double.

7. Divide into 8 portions and roll out into desired shape – knots, buns, or sticks.

8. Arrange on 2 lined baking trays about 2 inches apart.

9. Allow to rise for 30 more minutes.

10. Coat with a quick egg wash before baking for 8-10 minutes until crispy and golden brown!

11. Serve warm!

Biscoff Cookie Spread Pretzel Bites

Melty cookie spread inside a pretzel bun! You heard that right!

Total Time: 2h 20m

Serves: 12

Ingredients:

- 1 package active dry yeast
- 1 cup warm water
- 1 tbsp. brown sugar
- 3 ¼ cups bread flour
- ½ cup cold milk
- 2 tbsp. unsalted butter, cut into 1 inch pieces, at room temperature, plus more for greasing
- 2 tsp salt
- 1 ½ cups biscoff spread

Instructions:

1. Preheat oven to 500 F.

2. Into a stand mixer, add in the warm water. Sprinkle on the yeast

3. Add in the brown sugar. Mix thoroughly and allow to bloom until foamy. This should take about 5 minutes.

4. Add in the flour, butter, salt, and beer, and continue stirring. On low speed, begin kneading the dough for a minute or until it forms a smooth ball. Continue kneading until the dough become pliant – about 5 minutes.

5. In a lightly greased bowl, place dough and cover with saran wrap. Set away to rise in a warm area for 90 minutes, until double.

6. Place dough on a floured counter and divide into 12 equal portions.

7. Roll each piece into a rectangle. Place about 2 tbsp. of biscoff spread in the center.

8. Pull the two edges of the dough together and pinch to cover. Ensure the spread is completely covered and set onto a baking tray.

9. Repeat with the rest of the dough. Place dough pieces 2 inches apart.

10. Allow to rise for 30 more minutes.

11. Coat with a quick egg wash before baking for 8-10 minutes until crispy and golden brown!

Custard Pretzel Bites

Delicious homemade custard makes for a wonderful filling for these pretzel bites!

Total Time: 2h 20m

Serves: 12

Ingredients:

- 1 package active dry yeast
- 1 cup warm water
- 1 tbsp. brown sugar
- 3 ¼ cups bread flour
- ½ cup cold milk
- 2 tbsp. unsalted butter, cut into 1 inch pieces, at room temperature, plus more for greasing
- 2 tsp salt

Filling:

- 2/3 cup cornstarch
- 2/3 cup custard powder
- 2/3 cup sugar
- 3 1/3 cup milk
- 1 tbsp. vanilla extract
- 1 1/2 cup thick cream
- 1/4 cup butter
- 3 egg yolks
- 2/3 cup pistachios (chopped)

Instructions:

1. Preheat oven to 500 F.

2. Into a stand mixer, add in the warm water. Sprinkle on the yeast

3. Add in the brown sugar. Mix thoroughly and allow to bloom until foamy. This should take about 5 minutes.

4. Add in the flour, butter, salt, and beer, and continue stirring. On low speed, begin kneading the dough for a minute or until it forms a smooth ball. Continue kneading until the dough become pliant – about 5 minutes.

5. In a lightly greased bowl, place dough and cover with saran wrap. Set away to rise in a warm area for 90 minutes, until double.

6. To make the filling, combine the cornstarch, custard powder and sugar together in a saucepan and mix well. Add the milk, vanilla, and cream. Stir over a low heat until the mixture has cooked and thickened. Add the butter. Cook for 5 minutes, continue stirring the mixture.

7. Remove from the heat and add the egg yolks. Mix well.

8. Add the pistachios and combine. Cover the custard and leave the custard to cool completely.

9. Once dough has risen, Place dough on a floured counter and divide into 12 equal portions.

10. Roll each piece into a rectangle. Place about 2 tbsp. of custard in the center.

11. Pull the two edges of the dough together and pinch to cover. Ensure the custard is completely covered and set onto a baking tray.

12. Repeat with the rest of the dough. Place dough pieces 2 inches apart.

13. Allow to rise for 30 more minutes.

14. Coat with a quick egg wash before baking for 8-10 minutes until crispy and golden brown!

Jelly Pretzel Bites

Make your own jelly or use store brought if you're in a hurry! The recipe works well either way!

Total Time: 2h 30m

Serves: 24

Ingredients:

- 1 package active dry yeast
- 1 cup warm water
- 1 tbsp. brown sugar
- 3 ¼ cups bread flour
- ½ cup cold milk
- 2 tbsp. unsalted butter, cut into 1 inch pieces, at room temperature, plus more for greasing
- 2 tsp salt

Filling:

- 1 cup strawberries chopped
- ½ cup sugar
- 1 gelatin sheet, bloomed

Instructions:

1. Preheat oven to 500 F.

2. Into a stand mixer, add in the warm water. Sprinkle on the yeast

3. Add in the brown sugar. Mix thoroughly and allow to bloom until foamy. This should take about 5 minutes.

4. Add in the flour, butter, salt, and beer, and continue stirring. On low speed, begin kneading the dough for a minute or until it forms a smooth ball. Continue kneading until the dough become pliant – about 5 minutes.

5. In a lightly greased bowl, place dough and cover with saran wrap. Set away to rise in a warm area for 90 minutes, until double.

6. To make the filling, combine the ingredients together in a saucepan and cook until the strawberries have been crushed. Cool completely.

7. Once dough has risen, Place dough on a floured counter and divide into 12 equal portions. Divide each portion into 2 pieces for a total of 24 pieces.

8. Roll each piece into a rectangle. Place about 1 tbsp. of jelly in the center.

9. Pull the two edges of the dough together and pinch to cover. Ensure the jelly is completely covered and set onto a baking tray.

10. Repeat with the rest of the dough. Place dough pieces 2 inches apart.

11. Allow to rise for 30 more minutes.

12. Coat with a quick egg wash before baking for 8-10 minutes until crispy and golden brown!

Baklava Pretzel Bites

Delicious Middle Easter inspired filling takes these pretzel bites to another level!

Total Time: 2h 20m

Serves: 24

Ingredients:

- 1 package active dry yeast
- 1 cup warm water
- 1 tbsp. brown sugar
- 3 ¼ cups bread flour
- ½ cup cold milk
- 2 tbsp. unsalted butter, cut into 1 inch pieces, at room temperature, plus more for greasing
- 2 tsp salt
- ½ cup chopped walnuts
- ½ cup chopped pistachios
- ½ cup honey

Instructions:

1. Preheat oven to 500 F.

2. Into a stand mixer, add in the warm water. Sprinkle on the yeast

3. Add in the brown sugar. Mix thoroughly and allow to bloom until foamy. This should take about 5 minutes.

4. Add in the flour, butter, salt, and beer, and continue stirring. On low speed, begin kneading the dough for a minute or until it forms a smooth ball. Continue kneading until the dough become pliant – about 5 minutes.

5. In a lightly greased bowl, place dough and cover with saran wrap. Set away to rise in a warm area for 90 minutes, until double.

6. To make the filling, combine the nuts and honey. Set aside.

7. Once dough has risen, Place dough on a floured counter and divide into 12 equal portions. Further divide each portion into 2 pieces for a total of 24 pieces.

8. Roll each piece into a rectangle. Place about a tbsp. of nut mixture in the center.

9. Pull the two edges of the dough together and pinch to cover. Ensure the filling is completely covered and set onto a baking tray.

10. Repeat with the rest of the dough. Place dough pieces 2 inches apart.

11. Allow to rise for 30 more minutes.

13. Coat with a quick egg wash before baking for 8-10 minutes until crispy and golden brown!

Mascarpone and Fig Pretzel Bites

Looking for a unique appetizer? Try out these delicious pretzel bites!

Total Time: 2h 40m

Serves: 12

Ingredients:

- 1 package active dry yeast
- 1 cup warm water
- 1 tbsp. brown sugar
- 3 ¼ cups bread flour
- ½ cup cold milk
- 2 tbsp. unsalted butter, cut into 1 inch pieces, at room temperature, plus more for greasing
- 2 tsp salt
- 1 ½ cup mascarpone cheese, whipped
- ½ cup fig slices

Instructions:

1. Preheat oven to 500 F.

2. Into a stand mixer, add in the warm water. Sprinkle on the yeast

3. Add in the brown sugar. Mix thoroughly and allow to bloom until foamy. This should take about 5 minutes.

4. Add in the flour, butter, salt, and beer, and continue stirring. On low speed, begin kneading the dough for a minute or until it forms a smooth ball. Continue kneading until the dough become pliant – about 5 minutes.

5. In a lightly greased bowl, place dough and cover with saran wrap. Set away to rise in a warm area for 90 minutes, until double.

6. Roll each piece into a rectangle. Place about 2 tbsp. of mascarpone in the center and top with 1 fig slice.

7. Pull the two edges of the dough together and pinch to cover. Ensure the filling is completely covered and set onto a baking tray.

8. Repeat with the rest of the dough. Place dough pieces 2 inches apart.

9. Allow to rise for 30 more minutes.

10. Coat with a quick egg wash before baking for 8-10 minutes until crispy and golden brown!

Crunchy Cheesy Pretzel Bites

This one's a bit of a wild card but ABSOLUTELY delicious! Kids are going to love it!

Total Time: 2h 30m

Serves: 12

Ingredients:

- 1 package active dry yeast
- 1 cup warm water
- 1 tbsp. brown sugar
- 3 ¼ cups bread flour
- ½ cup cold milk
- 2 tbsp. unsalted butter, cut into 1 inch pieces, at room temperature, plus more for greasing
- 2 tsp salt
- 1 ½ cup grated cheddar
- 1 cup crushed chips of your choice

Instructions:

1. Preheat oven to 500 F.

2. Into a stand mixer, add in the warm water. Sprinkle on the yeast

3. Add in the brown sugar. Mix thoroughly and allow to bloom until foamy. This should take about 5 minutes.

4. Add in the flour, butter, salt, and beer, and continue stirring. On low speed, begin kneading the dough for a minute or until it forms a smooth ball. Continue kneading until the dough become pliant – about 5 minutes.

5. In a lightly greased bowl, place dough and cover with saran wrap. Set away to rise in a warm area for 90 minutes, until double. Divide into 12 pieces.

6. Roll each piece into a rectangle. Place about 2 tbsp. of grated cheese in the center and top with about a tbsp of crushed chips.

7. Pull the two edges of the dough together and pinch to cover. Ensure the filling is completely covered and set onto a baking tray.

8. Repeat with the rest of the dough. Place dough pieces 2 inches apart.

9. Allow to rise for 30 more minutes.

10. Coat with a quick egg wash before baking for 8-10 minutes until crispy and golden brown!

Conclusion

And there we have it! 30 fun and creative pretzel recipes for you to try out. Chocolatey, savory or a combination of sweet and salty, we've got it all! And now, so do you! We truly hope you've enjoyed this book as much as we've had creating it!

About the Author

A native of Indianapolis, Indiana, Valeria Ray found her passion for cooking while she was studying English Literature at Oakland City University. She decided to try a cooking course with her friends and the experience changed her forever. She enrolled at the Art Institute of Indiana which offered extensive courses in the culinary Arts. Once Ray dipped her toe in the cooking world, she never looked back.

When Valeria graduated, she worked in French restaurants in the Indianapolis area until she became the head chef at one of the 5-star establishments in the area. Valeria's attention to taste and visual detail caught the eye of a local business person who expressed an interest in publishing her recipes. Valeria began her secondary career authoring cookbooks and e-books which she tackled with as much talent and gusto as her first career. Her passion for food leaps off the page of her books which have colourful anecdotes and stunning pictures of dishes she has prepared herself.

Valeria Ray lives in Indianapolis with her husband of 15 years, Tom, her daughter, Isobel and their loveable Golden Retriever, Goldy. Valeria enjoys cooking special dishes in her large, comfortable kitchen where the family gets involved in preparing meals. This successful, dynamic chef is an inspiration to culinary students and novice cooks everywhere.

••••••••• ● ● ● ● ● ● •••••••

Author's Afterthoughts

Thank you for Purchasing my book and taking the time to read it from front to back. I am always grateful when a reader chooses my work and I hope you enjoyed it!

With the vast selection available online, I am touched that you chose to be purchasing my work and take valuable time out of your life to read it. My hope is that you feel you made the right decision.

I very much would like to know what you thought of the book. Please take the time to write an honest and informative review on Amazon.com. Your experience and opinions will be of great benefit to me and those readers looking to make an informed choice.

With much thanks,

Valeria Ray

Made in the USA
Columbia, SC
19 December 2019

85293376R00067